have the legs for it...

First published in Fontana Lions 1985
by William Collins Sons & Co Ltd
8 Grafton Street, London W1

Copyright © Text Lesley Cunliffe and Karen Usborne 1985
© Illustrations Karen Usborne 1985

Printed in Great Britain
by William Collins Sons & Co Ltd, Glasgow

Lesley Cunliffe
and Karen Usborne

My Passport
to France

Illustrated by Karen Usborne

Fontana Lions

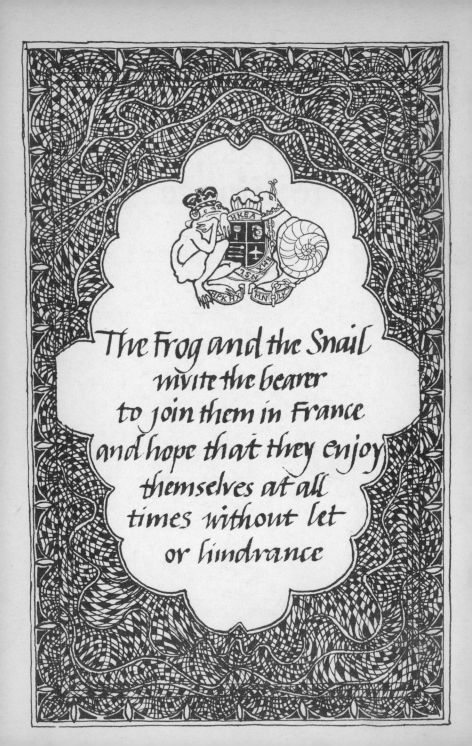

The Frog and the Snail
invite the bearer
to join them in France
and hope that they enjoy
themselves at all
times without let
or hindrance

Afford the Bearer more pocket money

MY PASSPORT TO FRANCE

without this book you would have to
worry about how to amuse yourself

Name of bearer _Simon Merrell_
Nom du titulaire

Accompanied by _____
Accompagné de

and by _____ grown-ups
et de *parents*

National status _English_
Nationalité

No. of real passport _____
No. du passeport actuel

Blood Group _____

Address of where you are staying _____

_____

_____

Telephone number _____

THIS BOOK MUST NOT FALL INTO ENEMY HANDS

DESCRIPTION *SIGNALEMENT*

	Bearer *Titulaire*	Friend *Ami(e)*
Date of Birth *Date de naissance*	31.0.70	
Hobby *Passetemps*		
Residence *Residence*		
Height (normal)		
Height (when you stand on tiptoe)		
Waist measurement (normal)		
Waist measurement (sticking your tummy out)		
Bicep measurement (normal)		
Bicep measurement (trying harder)		
Colour of eyes	Brown	
Colour of hair	Brown	
Scars & distinguishing marks		
Favourite pop group		
Can you do the splits?	Yes	
Are you double-jointed?	No	
Other talents		
Most hated food	stew	
Favourite football team		
Length of time you can hold your breath	1min 20secs	

Thumb Print   Photo

Bearer
Titulaire

Thumb Print   Photo

Friend
Ami(e)

Personal code word ___ ME REST EAT ___

PETS

Name *Nom*	**Date of birth** *Date de naissance*	**Sex** *Sexe*
Charlie	?	M

Usual signature of bearer ___ Simon Nemell ___

Unusual signature of bearer ___ [signature] ___

The bearer is requested to buy another book for his friend

INTRODUCTION

If it weren't for certain accidents of history, France would be owned by England, or contrariwise, as the Mad Hatter said. In that case there wouldn't be much point in going Abroad.

As it is, France is distinctly foreign, and full of mystery. The French are very stylish too. But if you meet someone who is being too stylish, just remember that French men used to go to bed wearing hairnets, and not too long ago, some of them wore lipstick and rouge. It is also as well to remember that the French will turn anything into an Art, given the opportunity. Food and drink are two examples. Love and gardens are another two.

And then they will argue about everything. Even tramps in Paris are connoisseurs. They argue over the merits of particular water fountains, and will go out of their way to drink from their favourite . . .

This book will help you with France's little ways and mysteries, and show you that sometimes things are not what they seem. It will help you be one step ahead, so you can enjoy France even more and feel on top of everything!

GETTING THERE

Let's hope you survive the crossing, and that if you go by ferry you won't end up feeling too cross. There are other ways, of course. Napoleon wanted to ferry his army across the Channel on giant rafts powered by windmills and invade England. Thousands of soldiers sat around in Calais while he figured out that it wouldn't work. Lucky for us.

Swimming across is always a possibility, even though the grown-ups will say absolutely NOT. Practise like fury for hours every day in the local swimming baths for about a year. Then smear yourself with several inches of lard and set off from the beach at Dover. This method is not practical if you want to take much luggage.

One man has been trying to reach France in a tin bath for the last five years, and is now suing the Coast Guard for continually rescuing him.

Perhaps a ferry is easier and safer after all.

The first thing to do on a ferry is look around, find out where the Space Invaders are, etc. Some ferries also have a disco and cartoon films. If not, you can provide a bit of fun for everybody.

Find a few sick bags. These are for being sick in if it's stormy and you can't make it to the loo in time, but they have other uses. You can make one into a hat, put two of them on your feet and walk around looking silly. Organise a scavenger hunt, and use the bags to collect all the things on your lists. A good list might be:

as many different beer mats as you can find
a French sweet wrapper
a grey hair from an old man's head
a red hair from a young man's beard
empty match boxes
an apple core
a crisp packet
a new friend who doesn't speak English (use sign language)

11

A couple of you could pretend to be buskers at the top of the gangway, entertaining bored people with your favourite songs. Or if the boat rolls a lot and everybody looks seasick, go to the buffet, which will be mostly empty, and try to make a House of Cards with beer mats. This will impress all the bad sailors and take your mind off things. If it doesn't *quite* take your mind off things, you could put a message in a bottle and throw it overboard. Put your name and address inside so that whoever finds it can write to tell you.

Go and look for stowaways. They are usually in the lifeboats under the canopy, or in the hold, hiding in a box. If you find any, make them pay you protection money.

The French part of your holiday is getting closer. Make bets on who will see the

coastline first, and see who can spot some of these:

Fishing boats (probably bringing in your next meal)
Tankers (for oil and liquid cargo)
Freighters (with cargo in crates and sacks)
Tug boats
Ocean liners
Colliers (loaded with coal)
Container ships (with cargo in big metal boxes on deck)
Fire boats

Dredgers (for keeping the harbour clear of mud)
Police boats (for arresting smugglers – extra points for anybody who sees a smuggler)

The ferry takes forever to dock, so while you are waiting to get off you can practise being French (lower your eyelids and shrug) and think of what your first meal will be.

That would be called the **cross-channel fairy.**

I wish someone would wave a wand and just get us there...

FRANCE AT A GLANCE

1. **Normandy**
   Bayeux Tapestry and
   the beaches where the
   Allies landed
2. **Picardy and Artois**
   Preserved battlefields
   of the First World War
3. **The Ile-de-France**
   The Heart of France
   and the Home of
   Kings
4. **Paris**
   The Eiffel Tower and
   Romance
5. **Alsace, Lorraine and
   Champagne**
   Forever fought over
6. **Lyonnaise, Burgundy
   and Franche-Comté**
   Grottos and sausages
7. **Savoy and Dauphiné**
   The Alps and wild
   flowers
8. **Provence and
   Languedoc**
   Film stars and fish
   soup
9. **The Pyrénées**
   Bullfights and Roman
   remains
10. **The Atlantic Coast**
    Smugglers, footballers
    and miracles

11. **The Limousin and
    the Périgord**
    Prehistoric cave
    paintings and truffles
12. **The Auvergne and
    the Bourbonnais**
    Viaducts and mineral
    water
13. **The Loire Valley**
    Fairy tale castles and
    Son et Lumière
14. **Brittany**
    Druid stones and
    magicians

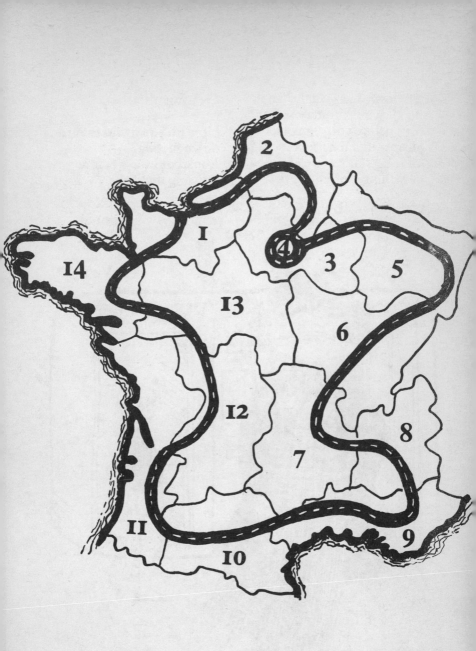

BEING THERE

So now you are in the land of food, wine, mystery and art. But before you plunge too deeply into the romantic side of things, it's as well to get a few things sorted out first:

Getting about

How do you avoid that run-down feeling?
Look both ways before crossing the road.

Look to the LEFT. French cars simply speed about with no regard for British lives and they usually come from the wrong direction, since for some reason they drive on the right-hand side of the road.

What's more, those things that look like zebra crossings (swots: *passage pour piétons* in French) are only fooling. If you step onto one and expect the cars to stop, they are likely to plough into you, and then you will have to shout '*Au secours!*' which is French for 'Help!' You'll have to be prepared to make a dash for it, even if the light is green for you.

Lavatories

The French word for lavatory is *nearly* 'toilet' . . . they say '*twaa-let*'. There are some very odd ones, so it's a good idea to know what to expect. You may be directed to the nearest Bar/Tabac. Don't worry if there seems to be no light: this goes on when you lock the door, so check where the lock is before you find yourself in total darkness. Sooner or later, you are bound to encounter one which doesn't seem to have a WC at all! This is called 'The Pit'; it is a hole with two raised bits that look like footprints on either side. The trick is to put your feet on these and crouch down. Be sure of your aim and remember that if you pull the chain before you step clear . . . your feet will get drenched when water comes whooshing out of the pipes. Don't slip when you race out.

Look for the new kind – much more fun. It's a sort of box standing all by itself, a bit like a Tardis, only with music playing and clouds of perfume. The doors open automatically after a time (in case you were enjoying yourself too much). Rumours that some children have stepped into them never to emerge (at least in this Time Warp) are untrue, or at least unproven.

There is another sort of public lavatory that only men use. It looks like a piece of sheet metal about the size of a bath towel wrapped around a tree, with a gap at the bottom, so that the feet and legs are visible.

You can take a guided tour of the sewers of Paris in a boat that goes under all the streets. It begins at a trap-door near the Quai d'Orsay, and it's really smelly. (see p. 64)

SWOTS: Some useful French expressions

It does seem a shame to visit France without communicating with the natives, so here are a few useful expressions to add a little *je ne sais quoi* to your holiday.

The following are cries of exasperation, and can all be translated as BOTHER/ RATS. Literal translations are given whenever possible.

Flute! (flute)
Zut!
Fichtre!
La barbe! (the beard)

Here are a few cries of astonishment, again with literal translations for your interest:

Ma foi! (my faith)
Sacrebleu! (sacred blue)
Sacré nom d'une pipe! (sacred name of a pipe)
Nom d'un chien! (name of a dog)

And here are a few useful expressions which you might not find in textbooks:

Oh toi, la barbe! Oh you, the beard i.e. shut up

Quelle moise What bad luck

Quelle barbe What whiskers i.e. what a pain

Je n'ai plus de friques I've run out of cash

Quelle cloche What a bell i.e. what an idiot

Les flics policemen

Allez, en route Let's get going

Que ca se grouille/Degrouillez-vous Hurry up

Qu'est-ce que c'est que ca? (generally pronounced *kekseksa*) What's that?

Salut! Hi!

A la tienne! Cheers!

Bon appetit (You should know this one already)

Ça c'est marrant That's funny

J'en ai ras le bol I'm totally fed up

Je suis à bout de nerfs I've had it

J'en ai marre I've had enough

Quelle barbe!

Money

You probably know that the French currency is the franc. What you may not know is that the whole franc system changed about twenty years ago: a couple of noughts were knocked off, so that 1000 francs became 10 francs. The idea was to simplify things (too many noughts can make your head go round) but it had the opposite effect, because a lot of people still think and talk in the old way. Typical French *esprit de contradiction* (contradictory nature). It's as well to know this, because when you hear someone saying 'mille francs' this could mean either 10 francs or 1000 francs.

The main coins you will see
are 50 centimes (there are 100
to the franc), 1 franc, and 10
francs. There are also a few
10 franc notes around, but
they are getting rarer and
rarer. Then there are notes
for 100 francs, 500 francs and
1000 francs.

French banknotes have
pictures of the national
heroes on them. The grown-
ups will tell you why they are
famous.

But you can tell them
something they haven't
noticed. Each coin has a very
tiny owl on it, and a Horn of
Plenty. These are the
engraver's signature.

NORMANDY

Hundred Years' War, when England and France greedily fought over who got what. William the Conqueror set off from Normandy to invade England in 1066 (swots: this was celebrated by the Bayeux Tapestry).

The Allied Armies landed in Normandy in order to rescue France from the Germans in the last war. So you can see that Normandy is full of History. The grown-ups are bound to tell you more of it than you could possibly want to know. This could happen when they drink Calvados, a very drunk-making apple brandy which should be bought from the farmer with the reddest nose. You should stay away

With its meadows and apple trees, Normandy was such a beautiful place that when the piratical Norsemen saw it, they decided to stay. That's how it got its name. Before that, there was Asterix and the Romans, and then the

from it. Drink cider instead.

The food here is so good that in the olden days meals sometimes lasted a week. If you have lost a bet and have to eat tripe, this is the place to do it. *Tripes à la mode de Caen* is a cow's stomach cooked with ox feet and cider and some people like it very much. As there are a lot of children who have never eaten tripe, it is a good thing to be able to brag about. The sugar apples in Rouen and the caramels of Caen might be more to your taste.

Mont St Michel is an abbey on a huge rock that becomes an island when the tide comes in. It is surrounded by quicksand, and lots of pilgrims got sucked in in the Middle Ages. There is something exactly like it off the coast of Plymouth called St Michael's Mount. Both of them are very ancient magical places of worship.

The Bayeux Tapestry

This was the first comic strip. It shows scenes from the Battle of Hastings (swots: 1066) with lots of people cutting off each others' heads and calmly trampling dead bodies underfoot. The French king, William the Conqueror, was so proud of beating the English on their own ground that he had the tapestry made to boast about his victory.

It looks a bit like this strip:

Canals

Most of France is criss-crossed by canals, particularly in flat, marshy areas like Picardy & Artois, where canal routes crop up everywhere.

Few people get seasick on canals. But canal-sickness is another thing altogether. You can tell someone has got it if he starts bossing everybody about like Captain Bligh in *Mutiny on the Bounty*. Since you can get just about anywhere in France by canal, they are quite crowded with such people. So here are some hints on how to avoid Madness:

Make your sister walk the plank

Fill balloons with water and have water-balloon fights with new friends

Have trials of strength by playing Tug of War on the lock gate bars

Make a one-man band out of the cooking utensils and give an evening recital

Dress up the boat with bunting, tell people you are being visited by the local gentry, and have one of your friends turn up dressed as a tramp

Dress up in rags and smear black stuff on your face and mess your hair

Shout to passing boats that you have been captured and are being used as a galley slave. If you can't speak fluent French '*à moi!*' will do or show them the page opposite

AU SECOURS

je SUIS ViCtIme DEs

BAnDItS

SAUVEz-moi

PICARDY AND ARTOIS

The peasants here used to walk about on stilts before they drained the marshes and turned each field into an island. Then they went about in pointy boats called *bateaux à cornet* which you will see if you go on a canal trip. You might come across some marsh gas pretending to be a ghost and you will understand why the peasants are so superstitious. A lot of the First World War went on here; pretty bad planning, in view of the mud.

On the Opal Coast the air is full of ozone which is supposed to be good for you and makes you slightly dizzy. Many French people come here for The Cure. If you get into conversation with a

French person, enquire about his health (swots: '*Comment vous sentez-vous aujourd'hui?*') since that is a subject which is very dear to them. Livers are one of their main preoccupations, and *crise de foie* (liver attack) is their most common malady, although the most widespread complaint is tiredness (*la fatigue*).

Some people say that Gothic architecture was invented here. Churches built in this style appear to be praying, with the tower like a pair of huge hands folded towards the sky. It was not easy to get this effect with heavy stones, but after a few churches fell down, they finally figured out how to do it; and when anybody thinks of what a church ought to look like, they are usually thinking of a Gothic church. The flying buttresses hold the walls up, and the big stained-glass windows look as if they are made of melted jelly babies.

You might see eels skidding across the fields in search of the sea. They are frequently interrupted, however, and end up in a local restaurant, stewed in wine. If you don't think about eels, this is delicious.

Otherwise, tell the others you are going to eat string and order *ficelles*, which is French for string, but instead of that you will get a delicious pancake.

THE V SIGN

Most people think this is a very rude gesture, but it is actually very patriotic.

When the French soldiers at the Battle of Agincourt saw how very good the English soldiers were with their long-bows, they vowed to cut off all the archer's arrow fingers – the first and second fingers of their right hands.

The English won the battle; and after that, whenever they saw a Frenchman, they would hold up their first two fingers as a taunt, to show they still had the upper hand.

CAMPING

Camping *à la francaise* (swots: in the French way) is an art in itself. Their tents and equipment make a camp site look like a canvas suburban villa. Whereas the Germans organize their camping life much like a military manoeuvre, the French have tents like miniature canvas châteaux. The English however (until recently) have always favoured the army type of camping, where everything is rough and ready, and if your feet stick out and it rains then you can always put them in a plastic bag.

There will probably be a lot of mud and rain and the object of camping is to avoid these. If you are asked to light a fire using only two sticks, make sure that both of them are match sticks. A good tip for drying damp matches is to run them through your hair before striking them. Even so you will end up with many used matches.

Here are some ideas:

1. How do you turn **ten** sticks into **five** without taking any away?

2. How do you turn **nine** sticks into **ten** without breaking any?

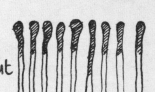

3. Take away **five** sticks to leave exactly **three** squares.

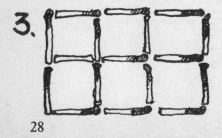

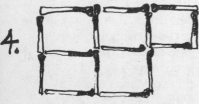

4. 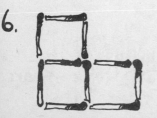 Remove **three** sticks and leave exactly **three** squares.

5. Move **four** sticks to make **three** squares.

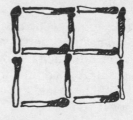

6. How do you turn this **L** shape upside down by moving **two** sticks only?

MIEPNBHGM ZN NSL LGA IO TSL UHHD

If you are the constructive sort you can also do interesting things with twigs. For example you can cut and sharpen lots of pieces of sticks about ten inches long, and make racks or shelves with them.

There are bound to be people who will join you in weakening the tent pegs. If you are near a farm, borrow a pig and zip it into the tent of someone unpleasant. The pig, it must be understood, is a clean animal and will probably not do anything it shouldn't in there. The look on people's faces when they come home, unzip their tent and see a pig calmly walking out will be the best thing you've seen the whole holiday. If you can't find a pig then a dog or a hen or a turkey will do.

Making apple-pie beds is an age-old pastime, and if you don't know how then follow the diagram. A good finishing touch would be to add a hedgehog if you can catch one. Avoid spiders, snakes or any other creepy-crawlies because they could put you in serious trouble. Be careful; the French sense of humour isn't the same as ours and you may get yourself in hot water.

The sites, you will notice,

have everything laid on. They sometimes even have a pool and a vine-covered restaurant terrace where you can sit and drink coke and eat ice cream all day if you want to.

You will have an opportunity of meeting French children at the camp site, so here are some tips about them:

They are very different to you. They are polite, resourceful, and old for their age. But beware! – when grown-ups aren't around they can be diabolical, noisy and cunning.

They have been brought up very strictly except for bed-times. They hang around in the evening for hours, pale-faced, exhausted and protesting – as you would – that they aren't tired at all really. They also have to work extremely hard at school. They must pass a ghastly exam when they are about seventeen called the Baccalauréat. Since they all want to go to University and learn how to riot, they try very hard.

Proper **Apple Pie Beds** need sheets: see fig:1.

Fig:1.

Fig:2.

For **sleeping bags, loose tacking stitches:** see fig:2.

THE ILE DE FRANCE

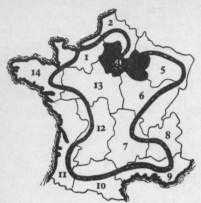

Versailles and Fontainebleau, since the kings and aristocrats preferred to live outside Paris. Rheims Cathedral is here, where all the kings and queens were crowned; and the Basilica of St Denis is where they were buried. Around Rheims are the champagne estates, where you will be allowed a free sample.

In the Château of Thoiry there is a nature reserve

This is supposed to be to Paris what the Home Counties are to London. The region is filled with châteaux and splendid palaces like

BE CAREFUL! Don't end up in the Bouillabaisse....

where you can see the wild animals roaming about the park. DO NOT GET OUT OF THE CAR. Lions are very partial to British children. Have you heard of the poem *Albert and the Lion*?

A more pleasant pastime (swots: *divertissement* – an important word) would be a cruise on one of the three rivers. That would be far more relaxing, and if you are going to Paris next you might need a bit of a rest first. Ditto if you have been to Paris.

If you do not like exercise and you are in the grip of grown-ups who do, now is the time to develop a mysterious ailment. There is a walkers' trail called the Sentier de Grande Randonnée (swots: the Path for Long Rambles) that encircles the whole of Paris. It is marked by red and white stripes on all the trees, and you may well find it is something to avoid.

THE FRENCH REVOLUTION
LIBERTÉ ÉGALITÉ FRATERNITÉ

If Louis XIV had not moved the Court from Paris to Versailles, the French Revolution might never have happened. At his splendid palace he and the aristrocrats were able to indulge themselves in all their expensive fads and fashions without seeing how much the people hated them. The peasants had to work from dawn to dusk to pay the huge taxes needed to keep the king in luxury. If they refused to pay they were punished by death, or a lifetime in prison, which was worse.

The king knew that things could not go on like that for much longer. His most famous remark was '*Après moi, le déluge*' or 'After me comes the flood.' What he meant, was 'This can't last long, but at least I won't be alive to see the horrible results of my silliness.' His son and heirs had much the same attitude. Louis XVI was on the Throne when the dams of resentment burst.

The people at Court had spent so many years having their every whim indulged that they were mad for pleasure and couldn't have changed if they had wanted to. France was bankrupt and half the population was dying of hunger. When the king's wife, Marie Antoinette, was told that the people had no bread to eat, she replied: 'Let them eat cake!' This either shows how ignorant she was of the state of affairs, or that she didn't care.

At last, the poor people took matters into their own hands. They stormed the most famous prison, the Bastille (swots: 1789). This was very satisfying, but there were only seven prisoners at the time, and two of them were simple lunatics. The real action began when six thousand women marched to Versailles, kidnapped the king and his family and took them back to Paris. And by then, Paris was being ruled by the people.

The Royal Family tried to escape but they were captured and had their heads chopped off on the guillotine, exactly as Nostradamus, the famous prophet, had predicted three hundred years before. (Swots: the

EBULKNL LRZEBNL OKZNLKGBNL

guillotine was invented by Dr Guillotin who wanted to find a painless and speedy way of killing people, since lots were going to be executed during the Revolution. He practised on sheep. The king was the first human victim of the invention, and Dr Guillotin himself, one of the last.

Louis XV succeeded his great-grandfather when he was also only five. Because of his easy-going nature, he was known for a long time as the *bien-aimé* (well-loved one). But he was probably the worst king France ever had - lazy and stupid and greedy – and some said that the country was ruled by his mistress Madame de Pompadour. He brought France to bankruptcy and set the stage for the French Revolution.

Marie Antoinette was the wife of Louis XVI. She thought he was a stupid failure and bossed him about. At their wedding there were wonderful fireworks. Unfortunately, one of them plunged into the crowd and 1,200 people were killed in the stampede. She loved pleasure and had a little model farm called Le Petit Trianon at Versailles, where she and her friends could play at being shepherdesses and milkmaids, wearing special outfits and using tools of costly design. All the lambs had bows tied round their necks. She wasn't at all serious about anything until the French Revolution, but she then showed remarkable courage.

French Snobbery

During the French Revolution, many elegant people were sent to prison. The most fashionable prison was the Conciergerie, and these people were terribly cross if they were not dispatched to this one. Rich prisoners were looked after by their own servants, and gave large dinner parties and lavish entertainment for their friends and other inmates.

LITTLE-KNOWN FACTS

Marie Antoinette and **Jayne Mansfield** had the same bust measurement.

The Ghosts of Versailles

One August afternoon in 1901, two English spinsters were walking towards the Petit Trianon in Versailles. They saw some people dressed in very old-fashioned clothes. Various odd things happened, and both women felt very low in spirit. When they compared notes, they decided they had slipped into the Past, 1788 to be exact, the year before the Revolution. They were both certain that they had seen Marie Antoinette sketching. One of them saw her twice more.

There were many other accounts of similar experiences by visitors to the Petit Trianon in later years; the most recent was in 1955.

So keep your eyes open when you go there, and if you see anyone in a frock coat, run up to him and pinch him. Ask him what the date is and get him to write it down for you. Open up this book and show him the message opposite.

(Translated, this means: 'We are from the Future. Leave Versailles at once. This is your last chance!')

38

NOUS SOmmES deS
RESCAPés De L'AVENIr.
QUiTtEz VERSAILLES
TOUT de suITe.
DeRNier AVerTISSmEnt!

After the Revolution

Things were very wild after the king had his head chopped off. Then, since you never know where you are in a revolution, quite a lot of the opposing team got their heads chopped off. A species of ghoulish women called *tricoteuses* (swots: knitters) sat in the Place de la Concorde and knitted a stitch every time a head rolled. There were soon enough stitches for a very long Dr Who scarf.

People who were not important enough for the guillotine were drowned by the bargeful, shot to the sound of music, and blown out of the mouths of cannons by the thousands.

The people found all of this rather shocking after a while, and decided to be rational. This brought some changes which were somewhat strange, probably due to the imaginative nature of the French. They decided to abolish tradition and religion, since these were reminders of the evil kings and the *droit divin* (divine right) that put them on the throne in the first place (swots: it was generally believed that Royalty was blessed by God, which meant they got away with practically anything). So the days of the week were

renamed to things like 'Billy Goat', 'Spinach' and 'Plow'. Because they were still fond of holidays the saints' days were changed to festivals in honour of the Pumpkin, the Turnip, the Pig and the Dungheap. Most of the churches were closed down or destroyed. The Cathedral of Notre Dame was turned into a Temple of Reason. An actress was put upon the main altar dressed up as Rationality, and statues of the best French philosophers replaced the statues of the kings of Israel, which had been mistaken for the kings of France.

And then Napoleon stepped in and pulled the people together by suggesting that they all fight the English and the Germans, and told them to turn the churches back into proper churches.

LITTLE-KNOWN FACTS

Napoleon was frightened of cats.

Louis XIV had a stomach twice the size of a normal man and he only took two baths in his life.

Both **Napoleon** and **Louis XIV** were born with teeth.

BASTILLE

PARIS

It is one of the most beautiful cities in the world – the *most* beautiful, if you are French. For centuries Paris has had a fascination, a style, a *je ne sais quoi* (swots: I don't know what) which has lured and enchanted visitors from all over the world. It also has a

NOT the Eiffel Tower...

joie de vivre (swots: irrespressible joy in being alive) which British visitors might find rather startling at times. As there are so many things to do and see here, boredom is likely to be the least of your problems.

As soon as you see the Eiffel Tower you will know you are in Paris. Go straight to a café and watch people being French. Have a little something to eat and drink as you do.

Observe a conversation between two Parisians. You will see to what lengths they go to defend their points of view. They always shake hands each time they meet. But this is a diplomatic preliminary. Before long, they will be flinging their arms about and shouting in rapid French. You can tell who has won by looking to see who shakes hands first when it is over. The French invented politeness.

They also perfected rudeness. The waiters used to express their disapproval of some customers by spitting in the soup before they served it (swots: according to the English writer George Orwell, who had a job as a dishwasher in a Paris restaurant).

The Eiffel Tower

It is considered quite spectacular to jump off the Eiffel Tower if you are committing suicide. Luckily this is very difficult due to the very high railings. As you already know, it is the symbol of Paris. It almost didn't get built because a lot of famous people signed petitions against it, saying it was too big. But up it went, and when it was first built anyone who climbed the 1652 steps got a medal. Once a Russian officer rode to the top on horseback. Do not try to do this. Instead you could tell everyone about the aerodynamical experiments Mr Eiffel, the inventor, performed. This means dropping feathers or paper aeroplanes from the top and seeing what happens. Fun, but before you think of doing this kind of thing yourselves it's probably worth knowing that a piece of brie once zooming down from the Tower was supposed to have chopped someone's head in half.

In the heat of summer, the metal expands and the whole Eiffel Tower grows six inches. There are still the same number of steps though; don't forget to count as you are going up. There's a lift for wets.

Since the Revolution Parisians have always felt they were stronger than king or government and ought to be running Paris themselves. There have always been plenty of people keen to join in whatever uprising has been arranged. When the city was re-designed in the last century the architect (swots: Baron Haussman) had a brilliantly spoilsport idea. He took note of the Parisian habit of rioting whenever they felt strongly about something. So he made many wide streets all leading off l'Etoile (swots: that means *star* and it looks like one on the map). Then, he said, whenever there was a riot they could put a large cannon on top of the Arc de Triomphe and fire straight down the streets into any quarter of the city.

In Paris the people celebrate with as much enthusiasm as they argue. This is particularly seen on Bastille Day (swots: 14 July, when the storming of the Bastille began the bloodiest argument France has ever had). Then there is dancing in the streets and everyone is

44

in a good mood. Be careful if you don't like being kissed. This is a French custom.

Cafés

It is worth pointing out to your companions that the reason French culture is so famous is that the painters and writers spent most of their time sitting in cafés, having arguments about the Meaning of Life. Suggest this subject whenever your grown-ups are running out of things to talk about. The French Revolution began in a café.

Bifteck et pommes frites (steak and chips) is a number one favourite dish here. Hot Dog and Sandwich are the same in French as in English, except that they taste better. Move your mouth vigorously when you order them, and it will sound as if you are speaking French. This applies to many things, so you should try it whenever you are stumped. *Croque Monsieur* is a toasted ham and cheese sandwich.

A favourite drink is called *Diabolo Menthe*, which means Devilmint. It is a peppermint soda made with lemonade. They also drink *Menthe à*

L'eau, which is bright green and tastes like toothpaste, and *Lait Grenadine*, pink milk. The best hot chocolate in the whole world is in France. There are lots of funny soft drinks in bottles with names like *Banga* and *Finlay* and *Pschitt*. Ice cream on a stick is called *Eskimo*.

French children sometimes drink wine with their meals, but their grown-ups always put some water in it. You may see a little drunken child from time to time. Trying out the wine is a good excuse to act silly and practise a few French expressions such as '*Je m'en fiche*' which is 'I couldn't care less'.

If the action flags, you can have a game on the pinball machine. This is called *les flippers*. Or try a game of table football, which they refer to as *le baby foot*.

Notre Dame

On the Ile de la Cité, one of the islands in the Seine, is the famous Cathedral of Notre Dame de Paris, where Quasimodo lived in the belfrey (swots: he was the star of Victor Hugo's book, *The Hunchback of Notre Dame*). Quasimodo was hideously ugly as well as being deaf and a hunchback. He grandly swung down on his bellrope to rescue a beautiful, virtuous young girl from the unwelcome attentions of a handsome cad. It is very odd that she wasn't deafened by the bells. This was in the Middle Ages, when there were public executions in the square outside, with the crowd pelting rotten eggs at the poor criminals who were being put to death.

Distances all over France are still measured from the Cathedral steps, so it is obviously the centre of the universe. When they were casting one of the bells, Louis XIV got all his Court ladies to throw some of their gold and silver jewellery into the pot, so the bell has a very pure sound. However it is no longer operated by a hunchback on a rope.

The Cathedral is made in Gothic style. It is supposed to make you think of Heaven, since it points upwards. This involved 'flying buttresses' to keep the walls from falling down. There are lovely monsters called gargoyles on the roof that spit out the rainwater (swots: gargoyle comes from the same word as 'gargle'). There are famous treasures in the Cathedral, such as the original Crown of Thorns that Christ wore on the cross.

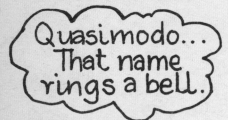

Quasimodo... That name rings a bell.

NAPOLEON

Napoleon got where he was due to the French hatred of the king.

You can easily tell who Napoleon is in paintings. He is much shorter than everybody else. He wore his hair in a fringe, and always stood about with his hand in his waistcoat.

After he had ruled for fifteen years, the country turned against him when he lost the Battle of Waterloo. He was sent into exile to a faraway island in the South Atlantic, where he died seven years later.

Eventually, France realised that he had been a great hero, and they brought back his body in great state. He was re-buried in seven splendid coffins in the Invalides in Paris.

If you go to Paris in the spring or summer, you can learn all about French history from the *son-et-lumière* (swots: sound and light) show at the Invalides.

After the upheavals of the French Revolution Napoleon, who had been a very good soldier, was invited to help run the country. Shortly after that, he crowned himself Emperor.

He conquered most of the other countries in Europe and then put his relations in to rule them as new kings and queens. 'One of these days,' said Napoleon's mother, 'I shall have seven or eight sovereigns on my hands.' This was a good joke, since

Josephine was Napoleon's wife. He made her Empress even though he was cross with her for flirting too much. But he soon divorced her and married someone else. She didn't mind though, since she continued to flirt

IZEBGAKHFL   ZUEL VZM B LKL B MZV LEUZ

and entertain lavishly in her country house, and Napoleon paid all the bills.

She was very superstitious. One thing she did most days was to go to her fortune teller, Mlle Le Normand, who wore a fur cap and looked like a monstrous bloated toad. Her consulting rooms had huge bats nailed to the ceilings. Napoleon put her into prison when she predicted his downfall. But she eventually got out and died when she was very old and very rich and still very ugly.

49

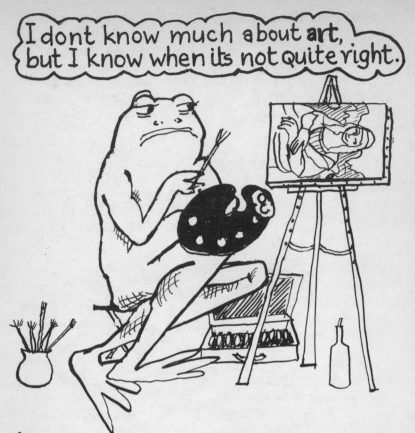

I dont know much about **art**, but I know when its not quite right.

Art

Mrs Grill is very ill
And nothing will improve her
Unless she sees the Tuileries
And waddles down the Louvre
(Trollope)

If you are lucky, your companions are not like Mrs Grill, who is clearly a person who goes in for 'sightseeing whether you like it or not'. Tell them that a little culture goes a long way, especially if it is someone else's.

The French are very big on Art, and there is a lot of it about. If your grown-ups are very keen on the subject, simply remind them that too much of anything is bad for you.

A good way to handle Art is to race through the Jeu de Paume, which is where much of the best can be found, and then go straight to a few cafés in Montmartre and talk about it. Regale the grown-ups with a few of your opinions. You can tell them a thing or two that they may not know, such as what Impressionism is, or Pointillism. (see p. 57)

Montmartre is where modern art was invented. All the artists lived a free and easy life here with their models, drinking and talking with writers and poets at the cafés and in their studios. This is where the streets are cobbled and the houses small and quaint, and there is a very nice graveyard full of dead painters.

If you want a good view of Paris, climb to the dome of the Sacré Coeur. This is a huge white Oriental-looking church. To build it stilts were driven down into the rock. If the hill were washed away by the rain, the church would stand on its stilts looking like something out of Star Wars.

The steps in front are used as a meeting place by young people who stand in small groups and eye each other.

There are still windmills and vineyards in Montmartre and it is a very pleasant place to go. The Can-Can was invented in Montmartre at a dance hall called the Moulin Rouge (swots: Red Windmill). Lots of artists used to come here to watch the dancing, which was rather daring. When they started ruffling up their skirts and showing their knickers, it became rather a famous dance. Toulouse-Lautrec, an artist who was only four and a half feet tall, used to draw and paint the dancers so he became famous too. His special favourite was a green-skinned redhead called La Goulue. (Swots: glutton. That should come in handy.)

Toulouse-Lautrec eventually died of drinking Absinthe which was such an interesting thing to drink that it was made illegal.

The Louvre

This is the French national museum and art gallery, built around one of the oldest courtyards in Paris. It used to be the palace of the kings until Louis XIV moved the Court to Versailles, when the apartments were then let to tenants. An artist colony gathered in the galleries, and in the colonnades little huts were constructed with chimneys sticking out through the elegance. Taverns and jugglers and other entertainers' shanties were built up against the walls and the whole place became very shabby indeed. Luckily, it was fixed up in time for the Royal Family to live in when the mob dragged them back to Paris from Versailles.

The plastic pyramid in the courtyard is an unexpected present from President Mitterand in 1984; he probably wanted to impose his taste on the place.

When you go to the Louvre, look for the initials of the kings and queens. In the courtyard, you can seen the monograms: K, H, HDB and HG; LA, LB and LMT. Guess which kings and queens they belong to, choosing from: Charles LX, Henri III, Henri de Bourbon, Henri IV and Gabrielle d'Estrées; Louis XIII and Anne of Austria; Louis of Bourbon; and Louis XIV and Marie-Thérèse. (Hint: in the olden days, some people used K in place of C.) The best one of all is the H with a double C. Henri II was very sneaky and combined his initials with his wife Catherine to form a D – which stands for his girlfriend, Diane de Poitiers. Champagne glasses were modelled on her bosoms.

There is a lot of art in the Louvre because Napoleon made each country he conquered give him works of art for the Louvre.

Louis XIV (also known as The Sun King) came to the throne when he was only five. He was a great lover of pleasure, built Versailles, and had many mistresses and children. He had lots of teeth when he was born, and only took two baths in his whole life – neither time willingly. His stomach was twice as big as anybody else's, but it was for his cleverness that he was considered the greatest monarch of all time.

Nostradamus was a sixteenth century French astrologer who wrote a book of predictions. He predicted the French Revolution and the rise of Hitler, and the assassinations of the Kennedys in America, (leaving one alive 'who would rule in vengeance'). He also predicted the end of the world in 1999: he said a great darkness will cover the globe and ashes will rain out of the sky. Catherine de Medici was his patroness. She fled from her favourite palace, the Tuileries, when he told her that it would burn down. It did, but not for two hundred years. Moral: Always press your soothsayer for exact information.

The Mona Lisa

At the Louvre you will see The Most Famous Painting in the World. It is the Mona Lisa by Leonardo da Vinci. It is rather a small picture of a woman with no eyebrows which was the fashion in those days (swots: 15th century).

She is smiling because it took three years to complete the picture, and the artist had people in to tell her jokes the whole time. But one Victorian art critic (swots: Walter Pater) thought she looked quite sinister. He wrote: 'She is older than the rocks among which she sits; like the vampire she has been dead many times, and learned the secrets of the grave . . .' You will notice that her eyes follow you around the room, staring at you and guessing all your secrets. Maybe Pater was right.

The painting is surrounded by bullet-proof glass and guards, because it was stolen by an Italian who thought she belonged in Italy, where she had grown up. During the two years she was missing, six greedy Americans each paid £150,000 for fakes that they thought were the stolen painting.

If the whole thing seems like too much trouble, ask them to let you wait in the car. You can see the Mona Lisa reproduced on tea-towels, ashtrays, postcards, T-shirts, and so on. Buy as many as you can. People love to get them as presents, because if you have a picture of the Mona Lisa it shows you are an art lover.

The Mona Lisa . . . On the opposite page is a colour-by-number Mona Lisa which you can turn into a picture yourself by following these instructions: Using a crayon or felt-tipped pen colour in the areas marked.

1: RED
2: BLUE
3: LIGHT BLUE
4: BROWN
5: PINK
6: LIGHT BROWN

Vive la difference!

IMPRESSION SUNRISE
It looks more like the morning after to me...

SOME OTHER JOKES

A frog went to the doctor:
'Doctor, Doctor, I keep thinking I'm a car.'
Dr: 'You must be round the bend.'

A frog went to the doctor complaining of still not feeling well.
Dr: 'Did you drink the glass of orange juice after a hot bath, as I suggested?'
Frog: '*Mais alors*, after drinking the bath, I had no room left for the orange juice!'

After a motorist ran over a small dog, he rushed over to the young woman who had owned it, saying: 'Madame, I will replace the dog.'
She said: 'Sir, you flatter yourself.'

Impressionism

You can impress people by explaining to them that Impressionism was a great break-through in the history of painting. It happened after photography was invented, and there was no longer a need for painters to record exactly what things looked like. The idea was to paint the effect of light or weather, so the Impressionists painted what effects they could see, and did not worry too much about what the subject of the painting was. Many people thought this style was messy and silly and they couldn't see the point of it. Several methods were used to give the 'impressionist' effect, including using minute dots of pure colour. These blended together when seen from a distance to form a completely different shade. That was called 'Pointillism' and the painter most famous for it was Seurat.

The name 'Impressionists' was invented by a critic who didn't like Monet's picture: 'Impression – Sunrise' (swots: Monet was a first division impressionist). But the painters took this term for themselves, and now their paintings are worth millions of pounds.

You can see for yourselves how it is done by filling in this picture in the manner of Seurat's 'The Bathers', with different kinds of dots. You could use colour if you want to, and then you will have made your own Impressionist painting.

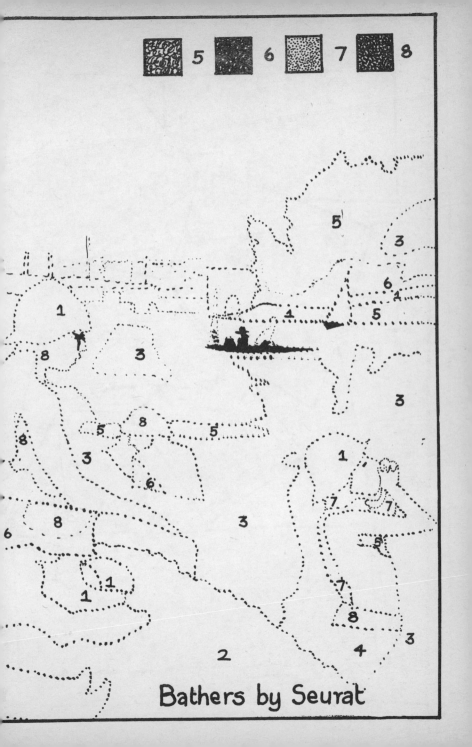

Bathers by Seurat

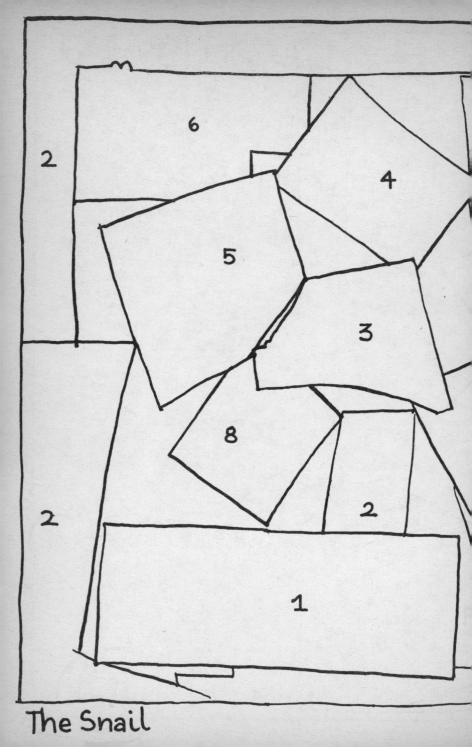

The Snail

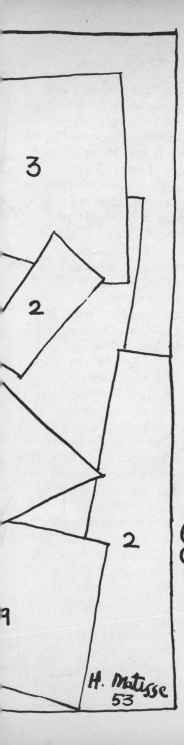

Matisse The scandal caused by Impressionism, and its daubed light or shade, was such fun for the painters that the next lot went even further and did away with shadows altogether. They used pure colour surrounded by black lines like a stained glass window. They were called *Fauves* (swots: Wild Beasts). Matisse was the leader of this group. Critics didn't know what to think but collectors were prepared to pay money for them so they either kept quiet or pretended to like them. Matisse wanted to make paintings into objects and not windows and produced this large canvas (now in the Tate) which gave up form altogether.

Colour it yourself using
1: Blue 2: Orange 3: Green
4: Black 5: Rose 6: Pink
7: Red 8: Yellow
9: Light Green.

I like it but I think it's upsidedown...

LITTLE-KNOWN FACTS

The first **Lift** was invented for **Louis XV** to get to his girlfriend's apartments on the floor below his own. It was called The Flying Chair.

Margarine was invented in France to replace butter for the 'poorer classes'. It was made from suet and pigs' stomachs and cows' udders, among other things. Modern margarine is not.

The first **Umbrella** to appear was used by **Louis XIII**.

The first **Restaurant** was opened in Paris in 1765. It had a motto over the door in Latin, which said: 'Come to me, anybody whose stomach groans, and I will restore you.' From the latin word 'restaurabo' in the motto, the word restaurant became common.

SOME OTHER JOKES

Young child in French restaurant: Mummy can I have some frog's legs?
Mother: Why? What's the matter with your own?

The Metro

When the Metro was built there was a worry that people would not want to travel under the earth, even if it was much faster. So they built splendid entrances that people would want to go into. These were made in a very French style called 'Art Nouveau', which is blobby and curly like jungle vegetation. The iron of the Metro entrances has now turned green with age, which exaggerates the Triffid-like effect. Many blocks of flats in Paris built at this time are so Art Nouveau that they appear to be almost alive. By using the Metro station entrances as a guide, you can impress the grown-ups by pointing out all the other examples of Art Nouveau you see. The style is associated with the *Belle Époque*, another way of saying the turn of the century. It is commonly supposed that everyone had more fun in those days. Ask the grown-ups to discuss whether or not this is true (swots: income tax wasn't invented then).

The names of some Metro stops commemorate extremely bloody incidents in French history. Even today there are seats marked '*Mutilé de Guerre*', reserved for men who have been wounded in the war. Most Metro stations have wonderful electronic maps for finding the quickest way to get where you want to go: push the button for your destination and the correct route will appear on the map in fairy lights. And remember that you have to open the doors of the trains yourself.

A lot of people don't know that the Metro is infested with pick-pockets. Some of the best ones are gangs of children under ten, who are very skilled. If you want to worry the grown-ups, say you've been asked to join a gang.

YET MORE THINGS
TO DO IN PARIS

There are masses of other things to do like **skateboarding** at the Villette Skate Parc, or visiting the **Circus** at the Circus Gruss near Hotel de Ville. You can take a **guided tour around the radio and television studios** at the Maison de la Radio; and if you **collect stamps** you can visit the Postal Museum.

There are **boat trips** on the Seine in boats called Bateaux Mouches. Don't fall in; the French say the river is so polluted only 50% of it is water. But you get a very good idea of Paris from the river.

Tour the **sewers** if you are highly motivated (swots: *les égouts* in French. It could come in useful as an insult). You get in to the sewers by a trap door in the Quai d'Orsay. When you are down there you can also send yourself a letter in a **pneumatique** which is a special vacuum tube that shoots messages across Paris in a few hours.

The **Catacombs** are very spooky. They stretch way under Paris. In the underground galleries are the skeletons of six million people. Nobody knows who they are since they all died during plagues or during the Reign of Terror and were thrown into mass graves. The workmen made gruesomely inventive designs when they piled the bones up neatly. Over the door it says, 'You are now entering the Kingdom of Death'. During the last war when the Germans occupied Paris, the French Resistance had its headquarters here.

There is a **dog cemetary** on an island in the Seine called St Ouen. It's not scary at all, with its little tombstones for Fifi, and Kiki, and Teddy . . .

Markets

Markets are wonderful, almost the best places to go to in Paris. They are free to get into and you don't have to buy anything. The grown-ups would be rather startled if you turned up with a baby donkey, for instance, which you could buy at the **horse and donkey market** on rue Brancion. At the **Flea Market** (swots: Marché aux puces) there are lots of funny old clothes and antiques. You might find something here that is a bargain. The fleas come free.

On the banks of the Ile de la Cité there is a vast **flower market** which is lovely to wander round. If you have some money to spare buy the grown-ups some flowers. This will make up in many ways for your dreadful behaviour in the past and will generally put them in a good mood. On Sundays the same place is turned into a **bird market** full of brightly-coloured budgies and whole cages teeming with little brown birds that squeak like flying mice.

SOME OTHER JOKES

What sits on a lily pad and says 'Cloak, cloak!'?
A Chinese frog.

How do frogs make beer?
With hops.

What can you make with two banana skins?
A pair of slippers.

Once an English man drowned in the Paris sewers. The French called it *Sewercide*.

Why are the Middle Ages called the Dark Ages?
Because there are so many knights in them.

Patient: Doctor, Doctor, everyone keeps ignoring me.
Doctor: Next please.

One candle to another: Are you going out tonight?

The Pompidou Centre

This is great! (Swots: another building donated by a French president, George Pompidou.) It's a building designed by an Englishman which has its insides on its outside. The French love to argue about it, so it must be a success. The best Art is going on in the plaza in front, where people come and do 'happenings'. It is a year-round circus with clowns, beggars on wheels, fire-eaters, people throwing flowers at each other, break-dancing, etc. Full of *inattendu*

(swots: the unexpected); you never know what will happen next. Cheer loudly if it is something that you like, and boo if you think it is not good enough. If you do this you will contribute to the making of an Art Form. Inside is a children's workshop where you can make sculptures or absolutely anything you like. Make a sign like 'Attention PLAGUE' which is a useful one for hanging on the doors of other people's hotel rooms. This will stop Room Service at least. Make a busking box and go into the plaza to try your luck (see p. 110).

NTRE:GEORGE:POMPIDOLI:

MIHN NSL ALEBULKZNL FBMNZDLM

Parks

Suggest going to the park. Grown-ups consider this appropriate on a visit to Paris. There are lots of opportunities for devilment, if you are in that mood, otherwise it is good clean fun.

BOIS DE BOULOGNE is a wood as large as Hyde Park and Epping Forest put together. There is a long race track where people go on Sundays. You can hire bicycles and boats for rowing on the two lakes. One of the lakes feeds a cascade like Niagara Falls which you can walk under. It is called Lac Inférieur. You'll never guess what the other one is called.

In the Bois there is the Jardin d'Acclimatation. It has a small zoo with a little farm, an amusement park, a dolphinarium, a miniature train and cars, puppet shows and so on. It is a good place to leave the younger irritants while you go stalking spies in the Bois.

If you are short of cash and you are bored, you can take up the hallowed tradition of hanging around lovers until they give you a tip to go off and buy some ice cream. (On the other hand they might tell you: *'Fiches-nous la paix!'* which means 'Leave us alone!')

BOIS DE VINCENNES has a very good zoo. If you need a rest the LUXEMBOURG GARDENS are a good place to go. There is a pool where you can sail model boats, and a little puppet theatre. Deposit your noisy sister on one of the antique horses behind the Punch and Judy. Then buy a hoop, and pretend to be a French child. Tell your companions that you feel you have stepped straight out of a Renoir painting. (Swots: Renoir was an Impressionist painter who frequently painted children looking polite and overdressed and rather pampered.)

Some other things to do in Paris

Paris is full of *divertissements* (swots: entertainments), so when it is time to take a rest from sightseeing buy a copy of the magazine *Pariscope*. This lists the afternoon discos for kids. Some even have rollerskating. There are cinemas with only cartoon shows, lots of swimming pools, ice-skating rinks, and museums that are such fun they shouldn't be called museums. Some of these are:

Musée Grevin

A waxworks museum that everybody loves, with mechanical people and scenes showing what Paris used to be like.

Musée des Arts et Métiers

Lots of buttons to press, distorting mirrors, conjuring sessions.

Palais de la Découverte

Science, space and technology centre where you can do your own experiments and play with all the machines. There are films and a planetarium.

Good viewing

MAKE YOUR OWN PERISCOPE

1. Get two cardboard tubes, one slightly smaller than the other.
2. Slice two inches off each one at an angle of 45 degrees.
3. Turn the top end round to make an angle of 90 degrees.
4. Stick them together with super-glue and tape.
5. Fit the two L shaped tubes together as in the diagram.
6. Fit two small hand mirrors in each angle so that they reflect each other. (This takes time but persevere). Use plasticine to keep them in place.

You now have a machine that can see round corners, over people's heads and into the window of the people in the hotel room on the floor above. You can expand and contract it by pushing and pulling it. To keep it in place when you have decided how tall you want it to be, stick pins or pegs through the two thicknesses of tube on both sides

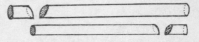

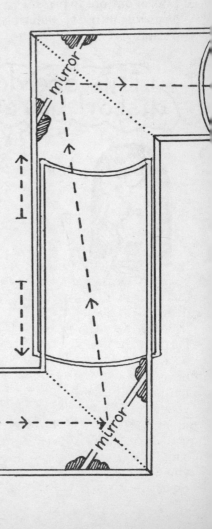

Ooh, la-la...

SPYING

Since the French are a secretive race, it can be rather good spying practice to follow one or two of them, and try to discover a few of these secrets. It will be necessary to look as French as possible for this exercise. You will notice that a number of them are practically identical in black berets and mackintoshes. A moustache is optional. Here's how to blend in to your surroundings:

Disguises

It is useful for a spy to change his appearance from time to time. If you comb your hair in a different way with water that has a lot of sugar dissolved in it, your best friend won't recognise you. Part it in the middle or slick it back. Put something lumpy in your shoe and practise limping. A pillow tied round your middle with a grown-up's jacket on top will make you much fatter. Add sunglasses and a beret and you will fool everyone, especially if you have been practising being French in the mirror.

Now you are ready to go into the streets and practise stalking. This can while away the hours nicely, and you will discover new and interesting places. Of course, it is lovely to observe people who do not know they are being watched. Wear plimsolls for sneakiness.

Keep to the shadows. You can stop and stare into shop windows and see your quarry reflected in the glass. Follow someone by walking ahead of him and use a mirror to look back. People never think they are being followed by someone who is in front of them. Stop to tie your shoes and look behind you if you think *you* are being followed.

Dead letter drops

You and your spying partner should decide on a few places to leave messages for each other. Good places are: cracks in walls, holes in trees, under sofa cushions, in a shoe in the cupboard, or under a special rock.

To signal that a message has been left in the secret place you can: wear your shirt inside out, leave one sock off, make a little pile of stones where they shouldn't be, or put two lolly sticks in a flower pot. Then the other spy will know to go to the dead letter drop, find the message and hold it over a light bulb, and decode it. Sometimes real spies tear the secret message into little pieces and eat it.

Secret signals

Learn these signals so that you and your fellow spy will be able to tell each other important information under the very noses of foreigners or enemies. Practise in complete silence. Motorway journeys are a good time. A little bit of giggling is a clever way of covering up what you are doing – BUT NOT TOO MUCH. Someone might interrogate you and force you to admit what the code is. This must not happen.

If you are signalling away in a street or other public places, do be careful that the French don't think you are just being very French. They might start gesticulating back at you and then things could get very confused. This applies especially in restaurants, as it may make you extremely unpopular with the waiters.

Codes and secret messages

The best invisible ink for secret messages is milk. When you hold the paper over a very hot light bulb the words will turn brown. But what if an enemy gets hold of the secret message? Then you will wish you had written it in code. You could make up a code book. Make a list of all the words you often use in your secret messages, and next to each put a silly word, like VAMPIRE next to LUNCH. So a secret message might read: 'Meet you after VAMPIRE'. That would fool anyone.

You could also use the Alphabet in One Phrase Code. Practise it by decoding the message on the Passport cover between the Frog and the Snail. There are other coded messages in this book for you to translate. As soon as you have uncoded a message you must immediately destroy it.

ZUT ALORS

ALSACE LORRAINE & CHAMPAGNE

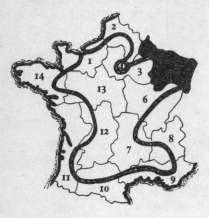

the poor goose with a funnel until its liver (from the goose point of view) is not at all in good shape. Sometimes they nail its feet to the floor so that it can't struggle or take any exercise. The French are not sentimental about animals. They eat horsemeat too, bought from special shops with a horse's head for a sign.

When there is a festival in Alsace, all the little girls wear red and black flower-printed costumes with white frilly blouses and enormous black silk bows in their hair – which makes them look as if a

Although France took Alsace from Germany a very long time ago, some of the names, the buildings and the food are still very Germanic. STRASBOURG has rather a German name; it is full of narrow little houses with such steep roofs that sometimes there are as many as five storeys tucked into one roof with their windows sticking out. The best *pâté de foie gras* comes from here. It is a particularly French kind of pâté, made from swollen geese livers; the French are very good at thinking up really fiendish things to do to birds. In this case they feed

giant black crow has landed on their heads, flapping its wings. The boys wear dear little black velvet suits with red waistcoats. Neither the boys nor the girls seem to mind wearing these things.

Munster cheese is made here, and it's the sort of thing you should avoid buying if you are travelling by car. It smells dreadful. If your companions really want some, make them send it home by post. It can have its uses, however; for example it can guarantee you privacy in a railway carriage.

You can also eat *kugelhopf*, which aren't smelly. They are sweet cakes baked in moulds so that they come out looking like ducks, rabbits or cows.

The grown-ups will be drinking kirsch, which is made from cherries. Try to persuade them to go to Alsace during the grape harvest. The Alsatians love to celebrate this, and there are many spontaneous parties in the wine growing areas. If you want to be popular, don't ask an Alsatian why he isn't a dog.

Let them eat Caviar.

Champagne is a bubbly white wine that people drink to make them feel light-headed and silly. They probably don't know that it is made where the bloodiest wars in all of France were fought. For centuries now, people in this region and in neighbouring Alsace have been expecting any day to have to stop being French and to start being German. Sometimes it was the other way round. Treaties have constantly been drawn and re-drawn to sort things out but nobody has ever been quite satisfied. This is because the French drink wine and the Germans drink beer, and nobody likes to change his tipple just because politicians or kings say so. The drink question at least was very nearly solved when all the vines caught a deadly disease called phylloxera. But they found that the grape vines in California were immune to it, and replanted all the vineyards.

When the grown-ups aren't drinking champagne, they will be drinking plum brandy called Mirabelle, so you won't have to worry about them (until the next morning). Then you will have them slightly at your mercy.

Lorraine's most famous person is JOAN OF ARC, who is the national heroine of France because she stopped it being English. You can still see the cottage where she was born, in Domremy. She was the daughter of a ploughman. When she was quite young, she began to hear voices telling her she would one day save France. So she put on boys' clothes and went to the Dauphin to tell him (swots: Dauphin means either heir apparent or dolphin). He gave her a suit of armour and 500 soldiers with which she defeated the English. But even though she was at the Dauphin's side when he was crowned king, he wouldn't ransom her when she was stolen by the English out of revenge. The English said she was a witch and burnt her at the stake. Then the French made her a saint. *Mieux vaut tard que jamais* as they say (swots: better late than never).

In winter, it is colder here than in any other part of France, which is good for the skiing. There are forests with woodcutters and lakes with fish that make good stews. Another tasty thing to eat if you are camping is blue trout fresh from the lake

THE LYONNAISE, BURGUNDY AND FRANCHE-COMPTE

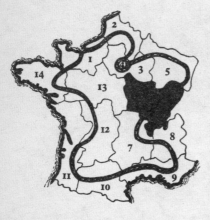

This is where the Jura Mountains are, with lakes and rivers full of fish waiting to be caught, and deep woods with rabbits and wild boar, wolves and bears. There are also huge chalk cliffs with grottos and vast caverns full of stalactites and stalagmites. (Swots: here's how to remember which is which – the stalagmites push up with all their **might** and the stalactites hold **tight** to the ceiling.)

There is a famous spa here called Salins-les-Bains, where the water tastes so horrible that the French are certain it is good for their health. A good way of starting a conversation here is to ask people 'How is your liver?' (swots: *'Comment va votre foie?'*)

If you travel through this area you will probably go through Lyons, where it always seems to be drizzling and the chimneys are extremely tall. Part of the city housed only silk weavers. One day they got fed up with working hard simply to make rich people look splendid, so they revolted. (Swots: 1831.) Soldiers were sent to bully the revolting silk weavers back to their looms, but they simply melted into the maze of little streets and left the soldiers standing around in perplexity. This same method was used by the French Resistance in the Second World War.

This area is over-burdened with vineyards, and the grown-ups will probably want to visit the source of the Beaujolais. This lies in Burgundy. (Swots: one of the cradles of Romanesque architecture; that is to say Early, Elaborate and Exhausting.) Tell your

companions that you want to see Veselay or Cluny vineyards which are particularly good ones. Notice how impressed they are with you.

If you like eating pigs then this is the place to do it. There is one sort of sausage that the local people like so much they have named it Jesus. You will certainly have to eat snails and frogs' legs here. Anybody who doesn't is a chicken, a quitter, a coward. Words of comfort: snails don't really taste of anything at all. They are like small bits of perishing rubber that have been drowned in butter after being asphyxiated in garlic. If you're in trouble try very hard not to think of snails you have known and loved. The same applies to frogs. They taste just like chicken. Try to visualize the cooked legs as a hinged wishbone. Make a wish while you're eating, and the fairies may grant it. *Who knows?*

MADAME TUSSAUD

Wonder woman in wax

Marie Tussaud was only six when she was sent to learn the craft of making wax models from her uncle. Once a doctor, he became a full-time sculptor when his wax anatomical models became a craze at the French Court. Marie was so skilful that when she was only sixteen she taught wax modelling to the King's sister. All the famous people of the day had their likenesses made in wax.

Wax heads of the Royalists were taken by the mob on the first day of the Revolution, and paraded through Paris for everyone to jeer at. During the days that followed, Marie and her uncle modelled the deathmasks of prominent victims of the guillotine. She had to snatch their severed heads, all dripping blood, out of the death carts. She smuggled them to her uncle's studio wrapped in her apron. Many of the heads were people who had been her friends.

When her uncle died, Marie inherited the business, and she took the collection of waxworks to London. Everybody rushed to see them on show in the Strand, where the Lyceum is now. The show, especially the new Chamber of Horrors, was so successful that she soon had a permanent site in Baker Street. Later the museum moved to Euston Road where it is now.

At first Marie and her uncle made most of their casts from dead bodies. Scalding wax was used to make the moulds. It was all such a gruesome business that horror stories like *The House of Wax* filtered from there into French folklore.

I hope they show my best profile.

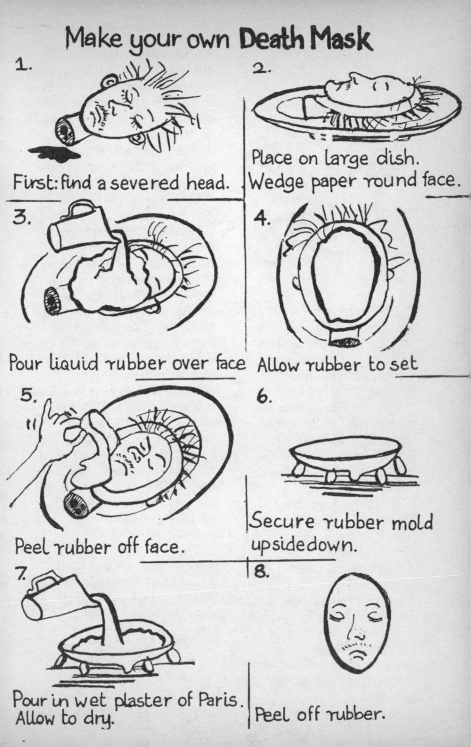

AUVERGNE

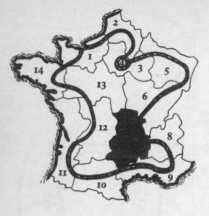

The Auvergne is a mountainous district with a magical atmosphere, with volcanoes and caves and strange rocky outposts. Anything might happen here. Wolves and Yetis have been seen in this century, and there are spine-chilling legends about what happened to people who went into the forest.

When the Romans occupied France, the fierce people of the Auvergne (like Asterix) held out for independence. Later it became a kingdom all on its own and produced two kings who ruled at the same time. (Swots: this was the 12th century.) Towns would compete by snatching relics of each others' saints and try to guard against them being snatched back. A town called Conques won the best of the lot: a gold statue of a saint called Foy which is covered with jewels.

The Romantic Movement was practically invented here by a writer called Honoré d'Urfé (swots: his novel *Astrée* was behind it all). He dreamt that his rich friends would look very pretty dressed as shepherds and shepherdesses in the spectacular landscape, so he invited them down from Paris and they all dressed up. The fashion caught on and for quite some time all of Europe was full of people trying, in an expensive way, to look like peasants. Painters loved it, and turned out lots of so-called 'bucolic' paintings (swots: this means pictures with cows in them). Harking back to 'the simple life' was recently made famous again by a dress designer called Laura Ashley.

There is another famous spa here called Vichy. The whole town is dedicated to Health, which the French worship, as you know.

The Wild Boy

A long time ago a wild boy was found in a forest of the Aveyron. He could only walk on all fours, and made no sound except for a high squeak in his throat. He had been abandoned by humans and adopted by wolves. A professor saw him in a circus and tried to civilise him. They became friends but the boy died. Nobody ever knew who his parents were.

> Now he wants a knife and fork...

XHP TZGN NLZTS Z GLV
AHR HEA NKBTDM

French Literature and their Heroes

The French are especially keen on books and writers; you can tell this by looking at their banknotes. Whereas English banknotes show heroes such as Florence Nightingale and the Duke of Wellington, the French ones show four writers: Corneille, Racine, Voltaire and Pascal.

The French think they invented modern literature with the *Roman de la Rose* and the sung poems of the Troubadours. These were about knightly love and duty (swots: the most famous was called the *Chanson de Roland*). Chaucer latched on to these and started the whole thing in English.

Plays have always been very exciting in France, especially as they are not very polite about the government. In fact the government was so worried about this that they created the Académie Française (swots: 1635) which was supposed to tell the writers what to say. The most recent thing the Académie tried to do was to tell people to stop using English words. But the French (understandably) find these so convenient that

(characteristically) they have ignored this ruling and every day blithely continue to use words like 'stop' and 'shopping'.

In the 19th century, the whole of French literature was turned upside-down by Guillaume Apollinaire, who thought he could get into his own mind with automatic writing. After that there was no end of weird ideas from the Stream of Consciousness, whose high priest was Proust. Then came Camus, who insisted that life was meaningless; and Sartre who invented Existentialism (swots: this means 'I exist because I exist and the same applies to everything else.'). Robbe-Grillet then invented

the novel without shape or plot, and Samuel Beckett, writing in French and then translating it into English, astonished everyone with plays that were almost silent.

Before long, there is bound to be a fashion in French literature for high and unlikely adventure. Future historians will no doubt put this down to the influence of Tintin and Asterix.

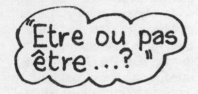

Honoré de Balzac planned 143 novels to illustrate the Human Comedy of French Life in the 19th century, and managed to write 80 of them in spite of the time it must have taken him to eat every day. He ate 110 oysters, 2 partridges, a duck, 12 cutlets, 12 pears and dessert at one meal. He was usually in debt.

Jean-Paul Sartre was a philosopher who invented Existentialism. He therefore started Beatniks and Punks. His girlfriend, **Simone de Beauvoir**, invented Women's Lib. This happened in cafés on the Left Bank.

Alexandre Dumas wrote *The Three Musketeers*. But he suffered from insomnia and his doctor ordered as a cure that he eat an apple every morning at 7 o'clock while standing beneath the Arc de Triomphe.

Victor Hugo wrote *The Hunchback of Notre Dame*. The French nation loved him so much that when he died his body was laid under the Arc de Triomphe and guarded by twelve young poets, and two million people went to his funeral. The French are a very dramatic race

87

SAVOY AND DAUPHINE

This is where the mountains grow up and become the Alps, and where France stops and Switzerland begins. The Romantics (swots: e.g. Keats, Shelley, Rousseau) decided the mountains were beautiful and wrote a great deal about them. In this century people also discovered they were useful, and skiing was invented. So if you are here, it's possible you or your companions are into 'Les Sports d'Hiver' or winter sports.

St Bernard lived here in the 10th century and ran a rest house for travellers. He'd go into the snow looking for people to rescue. It was years before some bright spark thought of using dogs with little barrels of brandy tied round their necks, but when they did they named them after St Bernard.

The mountains also used to be full of nimble ibex. Their legs on one side of their bodies are shorter than the other two, which explains why they are so good at running around mountains. There are still a few so keep your eyes open.

Smoked and dried foods are the speciality of this region. Meats such as ham and beef are often smoked, then hung in the forests to dry in the wind. All sorts of mushrooms are also put in the food. You will probably survive! The grown-ups will be drinking Chartreuse. This is made from a secret recipe

You're on the wrong mountain. This one's left to right...

by monks in the mountains. They will show you around the distillery if you want. Full marks if you find out the secret recipe.

At Annecy in June there is an international festival of cartoon films. If you are lucky your grown-ups will like that sort of thing. Otherwise it could well be just one wildflower after another, or alp after alp: Excellent for your yodelling.

hic

hic

THE COTE D'AZUR PROVENCE AND LANGUEDOC

This is the Mediterranean coast, where it is warm all the year round. It has beautiful beaches, some of them full of nearly naked people. English people have always come to France if they wanted to have more fun than was thought quite proper, or if they'd already had too much fun and couldn't pay for it. In those days it was cheaper than it is now. So many English people came to Nice that the best street was named the Promenade des Anglais. Nice does not mean 'nice', but 'victorious' (swots: *Niké* is the Greek word for 'victory', and it was they who named it). This is where people hope to be victorious in the casinos, where gambling goes on almost all night long. The same applies to Cannes and Monte Carlo, which are further along the coast towards Italy.

St Tropez was once a pirates' stronghold, and then a fishing village. Now it is a tourist trap, so keep away unless you own a yacht. The actress Brigitte Bardot lives here and everybody tries to catch a glimpse of her. She goes out every day to feed dozens of cats, some of which are descended from those owned by Colette. She was a famous writer who wrote charming books about

schoolgirls, young men and animals.

If your companions are musical then you are bound to go to Aix-en-Provence for some time, but that's all right since it is supposed to be the most beautiful town in France (apart from Paris of

course). Nearby is Marseilles, where you will be told to eat fish soup called *bouillabaisse*. This is made by stewing together every kind of creature they can fish out of the bay, including squid. It's surprisingly delicious if you don't look too closely.

Many artists came to paint the charming villages in the countryside behind the coastal strip. This is called the *arrière-pays*. Van Gogh painted some of his most beautiful pictures here before he went mad and cut off his ear. Part of his problem might have been the wind. If you want to get off going somewhere, tell the grown-ups that you are allergic to the Mistral. Remind them of Van Gogh. The Mistral is a famous wind that blows in from Africa and makes everybody bad-tempered. Even if it isn't actually blowing, you can say that you feel as if it's starting up,

which cannot be argued with.

Arles has a huge old Roman amphitheatre where Christians were thrown to the lions. Nowadays all you'll see there is some poor old bull being driven mad. The place is littered with Roman remains. The mysterious Order of Knights Templar had their headquarters here. (It is now a museum.) They were considered to be heretics because they believed that Christ didn't die on the Cross, but climbed down and escaped to Marseilles where he married Mary Magdalene, had lots of children and lived happily ever after.

The Camargue stretches beyond Arles. It is a marshy plain with mosquitoes where the Mistral blows fiercely. You'll see pink flamingoes and mysterious wild horses roaming and a lot of gypsies, who aren't at all bothered by mosquitoes or the Mistral, and are very fond of horses.

I thought you said this would be fun...

Picasso

Pablo Picasso lived here and was, as everybody knows, a genius. A genius is somebody very like you, only older. He was the greatest artist of this century, and could pay for his dinners just by scribbling a little picture on the menu and signing it. He invented Cubism, which everybody found very shocking at first. It was done by putting all the angles from which he looked at something into one painting. This could make a woman's face look as if it had been shuffled like a pack of cards. Sometimes he painted the shuffled faces purple, green or yellow. It took some getting used to.

When he was only nine he was already such a good painter that his artist father gave Picasso all his paints and brushes and vowed never to paint again. Picasso was really Spanish, but he painted all his best pictures here and lived in the south of France till he died a very old man, so he is an honorary French person.

Colour in the painting on the next page using
1: YELLOW 2: BLUE
3: GREEN 4: RED

On the beach

Bottles with messages in them might have been washed up on the shore. It's a good idea to have a look for those straightaway, and then see if there is any buried treasure. If not, stroll around and see what there is in the way of treasure, and bury some. Make a treasure map of where to find it.

You're bound to find some Mermaids' Purses to pop (these are really the used egg-cases of skate and dogfish); and often there are lumps of cork that have drifted in from Spain. (Swots: in Olden Times people thought that cork prevented cramp, and strapped it to their legs; it's good for growing pains.) Beware of jellyfish and tar. If you are attacked by either of these, tell the grown-ups that ammonia takes away jellyfish stings, and eucalyptus oil from the chemist will get the tar off. Then just sit back and enjoy being looked after.

If you entirely fail to find treasure on the beach, you may still find a pearl in your oyster. It is a brave child who eats an oyster for the first time as they are rather queer and don't taste of anything other that sea water, but you might as well try them. The worst thing is that they are still alive when you start munching (or should be).

You can cover yourself in seaweed and march about like a creature from the Deep and terrify everybody. On some beaches if you did this you would be the only one with anything on at all, as the French often sit on beaches with at least their tops off. They don't think this is shocking. They are a very open-minded race, and call it healthy, and they could well be right. As we know it is highly embarrassing.

MZPQL JPB ILPN

Man with an Ice Cream Cone

by Picasso

Pirates

Another good game if there are enough of you is **Pirates and Politicians**, which falls into two parts:
You need two boats and at least six people. Each boat load has a treasure. This consists of a hoard of goodies, chocolate or anything else you may like. Add 100 francs to make the game more exciting. Bury the treasure. Each member of the crew then makes a map and hides it somewhere on his person. (Watch out at this point for spies.) The idea of the game is to catch one or all of the other crew and get their map from them. If anyone is pushed into the water they are automatically dead for ten minutes. Marks off for falling in; also for getting carried off by the other crew. The treasures must eventually be joined together and taken to a pre-arranged place which is the Bank. Your share depends on how well the rest of the players think you fought for it.

This last part of the game is called **Politics**. It can take longer than the first part, for you also get awarded marks for eloquence in another person's defence. It can be

played later in the car or at supper. If you're still friends at the end of this game, then you are friends for life.

THE ATLANTIC COAST

Although most of the Basques live in Spain, some spill over the Spanish border into France. They are an unusual race, believed by some to have descended from the children lured away by the Pied Piper. He was supposed to have brought them to France via Japan; and it is true that their language has some Japanese elements in it. In the olden days, they were all smugglers, pretending to be sheep farmers on the side.

Lourdes is where a little girl called Bernadette saw the Virgin Mary. Nobody else saw the vision, but they did see a rosebush blossoming at the wrong time of the year. Bernadette's vision led her to a spring, which is now channelled into pools that cripples and sick people jump into, hoping for a miraculous cure. Sometimes it works. Thousands of people go there every year. If you are looking for something to take back to your friends, buy a biro which has the Virgin Mary rising up or sinking down, depending on which way you hold it.

This is clearly one of the holy places of the world; funnily enough, however, it also used to be the home of the wickedest man in all of French history: Gilles de Rais.

Gilles de Rais was an aristocratic soldier who was Joan of Arc's companion at arms. But his real claim to fame is that the ogre, Bluebeard, was modelled on him. He was as wicked as wicked could be, and stole more than 140 children whom he spoiled with fine clothes and then tortured horribly. And after he had tortured them, he sent the poor children into the kitchens, had them roasted, and ate them for his dinner. *Pas très gentil* (swots: not very nice).

The most famous vineyards are in this region, and the grown-ups will not

only drink wine but also Cognac and Armagnac, which are two strong brandies. This could well mean that in the mornings you'll be asked to be extra quiet.

The onion soup (swots: *soupe à l'onion*) here is delicious with bread and cheese floating on top. Doves are stuffed with mushrooms and truffles and served on toast spread with pâté.

DORDOGNE LIMOUSIN AND PERIGORD

This is the famous châteaux country. If you are here, châteaux are likely to be the focal point of your visit; if you don't like them get hold of a good book and eat too much so that you have to stay behind.

On the battlefields of Poitiers the Franks repelled the invading Visigoths. (Swots: this was in 507. The Visigoths were part of the team that sacked Rome. They didn't do so well in France.) The Saracens tried it next, and if they hadn't been sent away then we would probably all be Islamic now and say our prayers facing East at sunset. The English won the Battle of

Poitiers here when the Black Prince captured the French king.

At Aubusson they have been producing tapestries for centuries. These have always been extremely swank, not to say expensive. You are allowed to go into some of the workshops and watch them and it is well worth the visit.

The mellow sandstone houses of the Dordogne are quite lovely. They were built at a time when French good taste was at its best. People often get a wild urge to come and live here, but don't forget the mosquitoes. See if you can't find traces of Dr Who around. He used to come here for his summer holiday every millenium or so.

It was here in the Dordogne that one day a boy was taking his dog for a walk. The dog vanished down a rabbit hole which led to a cave. Somehow the boy followed: imagine his surprise when he found himself surrounded by walls covered with extraordinarily beautiful prehistoric drawings of animals! This is Lascaux, and has now been closed because people used to breathe on the pictures and ruin them. If you want to see them for yourself you will have to become a swot and get a degree in Archaeology.

THE MAN IN THE VELVET MASK
AND OTHER STRANGE STORIES

A long time ago a Frenchman was arrested and put into prison, where he stayed for the rest of his life, wearing a black velvet mask. He ate and slept with it on. Everyone was very curious about who he might be, since he was given every luxury and courtesy. It was assumed that he must be very important, and some thought that he was the king's twin brother. But no one could ever find out who he was. Later, some people had an even more interesting idea. He probably had a disease with a very long name which gives the sufferer red eyes and makes his lips draw back in a snarl to reveal red teeth. If the skin is exposed to sunlight it bleeds. This disease might have made him look like Dracula. It was all supposition though, and he took his secret to the grave.

In 1899 the rotting corpse of an unknown man was found in a trunk floating in the river near LYONS. The police managed to trace this trunk back to Paris. The head of the Lyons police discovered that the murdered man had walked with a limp and had had water in the knee. He also knew the man's height and managed to guess at his age; and finally all these clues matched the description of a missing man called Conffé. This was the first murder of its kind to be solved by the methods later used by Sherlock Holmes.

Frappe frappe

Qui est la?

Jacques.

Jacques qui?

J'Accuse...

This is funny only if you know the story of the Dreyfus Case. Dreyfus was a Jewish army officer who was falsely accused of spying. The whole country was divided as to whether he was guilty or innocent.

Emile Zola, a novelist you will be encouraged to read when you are a bit older, published a famous blast against the side that thought Dreyfus was guilty. He called it: 'J'accuse' (French for 'I accuse'.) In it he accused them of hating Jews and of gang warfare.

Elementary.... Emile Zola, without a doubt...

THE PYRENEES
AND
ROUSSILLON

The Pyrenees are the mountains that separate France from Spain. You will notice a sudden change when you go over the border. The Spanish customs officials all have moustaches and the ice cream is quite different. One of the best ways of giving the impression that you are very clever is to say '*pas dans le Midi*' which means 'not in the South'. It can apply to anything and usually does. If you say this and nothing else during a discussion about France, people will be *très impressionnés* (most impressed).

The châteaux and even the churches here were built like forts to withstand the Spanish and the Arabs, who kept trying to take over. A lot of bullfighting goes on here. People also like to play an extremely dangerous game called Pelote. If you stick around to watch, you may see somebody being killed by catching the small hard ball on his head. A completely harmless game, however, is *boules* (swots: a bit like our game of bowls, but not so rarified). Keep asking questions until somebody teaches you. The French play it all over France, but this is where it was invented.

Long ago people called the Cathars lived here. They believed the world was made by the Devil and rejected Christianity, so they were a natural target for the Crusades. Naturally they were exterminated. But they knew this would happen, so had cleverly trained the young men to sing songs (which they did at courts all over Europe) with secret messages in them. These singers were called the Troubadours and they would never explain their songs.

If you are very lucky you might go to Carcassone. The whole town is one huge castle, and you can join the French kids in a never-ending game of knights and ladies. All the moats and drawbridges are in working order.

You might have to eat garlic soup while you are here. A word of comfort: if you overdose on garlic, vampires won't touch you. A word of warning: nobody else will touch you either.

In Perpignan at Easter the holy statues are taken from the churches and paraded through the streets by men disguised in long black robes and conical black hats and veils. It's all rather weird.

SPORT

The French love football probably as passionately as the English do. But they never quite got the hang of cricket; it never caught on in France. This might have something to do with the civilised nature of the game; there's no room for violent argument in it, and the French like to get *surexcité* (overexcited) whenever possible. Even boules – their nearest equivalent to cricket – appears to be a reasonably peaceful game, but it is really their only way of resolving disputes and feuds, and in this respect is a substitute for duelling. Basically, it's like Hop-Scotch without the hopping.

They like bull-fighting in the South, but unlike the Spanish they don't kill the bull. Instead he wears a tassled hat between his horns and is allowed to run around the town while all the young men have a go at snatching a tassle or two off to give to their girlfriends.

Cycling, of course, is more popular in France than

anywhere else in the world. The great cross-country race called the *Tour de France* is usually televised worldwide. And nowadays most French sportsmen get their training by throwing empty beer cans at the television set . . . like the rest of the world.

Of all the games the French love to play, Miniature Golf has recently become by far the most popular. They have mini-golf leagues and take the whole thing very seriously. It helps to know the rules before you start: these are based on the rather obvious notion that the fewest number of strokes to get the ball in the holes win.

A good variation on this is Miniature Cheating golf, where you bribe someone to steal the other person's ball, or give a dreadful shriek just as he is about to putt.

SOME GOLF JOKES

Why does a golfer take a spare pair of trousers with him?
In case he gets a hole in one.

How should I have played that last shot?
Under a false name.

BUSKING MACHINE

This is light and portable. If you get moved on by the police (swots: *les flics*) pick it up and take it with you.

Instructions

1. Find a large cardboard box, the biggest you can get hold of – 3ft square or larger.
2. Cut holes on each side and on the top which are big enough for your head to get through.
3. Draw around the holes any designs you like.
4. Learn the words and tunes of at least four songs and practise them in the bath.
5. Crouch inside the box somewhere public. The Pompidou Centre is perfect. Get a friend to throw a coin.
6. Stick your head out and sing one of your songs. Taped backings help. Soon you will have a crowd around you.
7. Do not lose your nerve.

THE LOIRE VALLEY

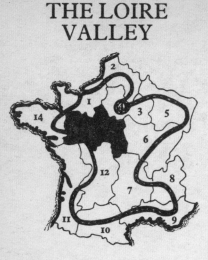

Here are the beautiful storybook castles, with grottos and towers, walled vegetable gardens laid out like patchwork quilts, fantastic fountains, artificial lakes on hills, châteaux on top of lakes, and fantastic things cut out of hedges.

The castles were all built for different reasons and you can tell the difference by looking at them. The massive ones on the tops of rocks are the oldest. These were built to keep enemies out. In those days, important men tried to prove their power by capturing the castles of other important men. It was quite a bloody business. The men who wanted to capture a castle would bring giant battering rams to bash down

the castle door, catapults bigger than you can imagine to throw huge stones over the walls, and flaming torches. They also invented germ warfare by throwing rotting carcasses over the walls, in the hope that they would start an epidemic.

Of course, the people inside the castle were not without tricks themselves. They would rain arrows out of the window slits and pour down boiling oil and horrible quicklime onto the soldiers who were scaling the castle walls with grappling hooks. But still the best way to defend yourself would have been to go and capture somebody else's castle, since the attackers usually won: even if the people inside succeeded in defending themselves (which sometimes took years) they would eventually die of starvation.

At last the kings became more powerful and told everybody to stop fighting and to build beautiful châteaux instead. These are the ones that are pleasantly situated on the banks of the river. Each tried to outdo his neighbour with the splendour and originality of his château and gardens. One garden has a series of hedges showing four kinds of love – tender, tragic, fickle and unfaithful. They were very keen on love, and spent all their time dressing up and playing at it. This was obviously better than war as fewer people got killed.

The idea was basically to have as much fun as possible, in the prettiest surroundings they could devise. But meanwhile the peasants were being taxed more and more to pay for all the beauty, and eventually they got so cross that they revolted and killed the king and all the aristocrats they could find.

But you've heard that one.

If you love me, say so but don't touch my castle...

THINGS TO DO IN A RESTAURANT WHILE YOU ARE WAITING TO BE SERVED

1. Arrange with your kid sister that when she touches her nose it means 'knife', rubs her ear it means 'fork', and scratches her chin it means 'spoon'. After you have ordered, tell the grown-ups that you are going to the 'twaa-let' but that you will know if someone touches your cutlery. Come back and tell them which one was touched. The trick in this lies in keeping in with your kid sister.

2. Fill a glass with water and put a piece of paper over the top. Carefully turn the glass upside-down, holding the paper in place for a few moments. Then let go of the paper. It will stay in place and on the glass, and none of the water will come out. If it does, you must have done it wrong.

3. With one quick tug it is possible to remove a tablecoth without any of the cutlery or glasses etc. being disturbed. But *attention!* This one needs a bit of practice.

4. In a glass half full of water, drop a piece of bread the size of the top of your finger. Then pour wine slowly on the floating bread. The wine will not mix with the water and the two liquids will stay separate from each other.

5. Tell the grown-ups about the Seige of Paris (swots: 1871). When the Germans occupied Paris, everybody was so hungry that they ate the animals in the Zoo. One Englishman went to a famous restaurant and all they had on the menu was kangaroo, horse, donkey and wolf.

6. Draw a picture on the menu and tell the waiter that you are a distant relation of Picasso. Ask if he will take the drawing as payment for your dinner.

7. Tell the grown-ups that people who were too poor to go to restaurants ate rats from the sewers. A newspaper actually published instructions on how to fish for rats:

> 'Take a strong line and a large hook, bait with tallow, and gently agitate the cord. It will be some time before the rat decides to swallow it, for his nature is cunning. When he does, leave him five minutes to meditate over it. Then pull strongly and suddenly.

He will make convulsive jumps, but be calm, and do not let his excitement gain on you. Draw him up, *et voilà votre diner.*'

Cats and rats were sold as food in the markets, cats for five francs and rats for only two francs.

They are bound to be interested to hear this.

If you see someone you want to impress with your superiority hold up the opposite page. Ask a grown-up to translate it for you.

Moi JE prEFERAIS.

TrOis etOilEs MichELin.

qu'eN diS tu?

BRITTANY

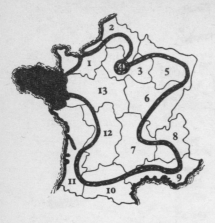

The Celtic name for Brittany is *Ar Mor*, which means Land of the Sea.

It is also the land of sandy beaches, rocks and pebbles, stormy seas (it feels like a true *champs de bataille* or battlefield when the winds start roaring) and lovely walks. The winters are mild, so the flowers and trees are often quite exotic. You can spend hours scrambling over rocks and into caves, cycling and swimming. The air is invigorating and relatively unpolluted. Enjoy the mussels, which you can gather yourself, together with all the other *fruits de mer* (seafood) which are likely to take up most of your eating time. *Crêpes* and *gaufres* (pancakes and waffles) are also specialities here.

As soon as you arrive, someone is bound to tell you about the great connections between Brittany and Wales. The Bretons speak a language very like Welsh. But the real

connection between Britain and Brittany are the Druids.

These were magicians who lived in ancient times. They told the people to build Stonehenge, and also the mysterious stone circles in Brittany, such as the ones which stand lopsidedly around at Carnac, like recruits from Dad's Army. One of the most famous Druids was Merlin. King Arthur made friends with him when he came to Brittany with the Knights of the Round Table to look in the forest at Paimpont for the Holy Grail. Your companions probably won't know that Tristan and Iseult came to a castle here after they drank the magic love potion that began their romantic saga. If one of them does, ask to hear the story of Wagner's *Ring Cycle*. It is a great sleep-inducer.

The Bretons are still more Pagan than Christian, as you can see from the Calvary which is to be found in every village. These are ancient stones that were translated into Christianity by being carved up to represent the Crucifixion, but the effect is really not very convincing. They still believe in witches and fairies.

You will observe that in each district the women wear a different sort of lacy hat, firmly anchored on by ribbons, as they have to be with all that wind blowing.

HOW TO ENJOY A HOTEL

First of all get a few supplies together. Stroll around the passages collecting the rolls, butter and jam that people have left on their breakfast trays. These will be outside their doors when they've finished.

They may also have put their shoes out to be polished. It can be amusing to switch them all around. This will encourage the other guests to make friends.

Listening through walls can be very interesting. Get an empty glass and put the open end to the wall where the sounds are coming through. If nothing very much is happening, turn the glass around. Put the bottom end to the wall and moan horribly through the open end. The people next door will think they have been given the haunted room.

If you are punished for anything, make paper darts with messages in them. The message should read something like: 'Am being held prisoner against my will. Please bring help.' (Swots: '*Je suis captif. Au secours,*' will do.) Throw them out of the window and await results.

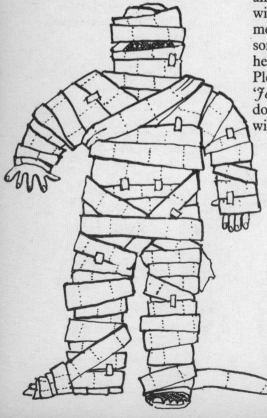

What does a monster call its parents?

Dead and Mummy.

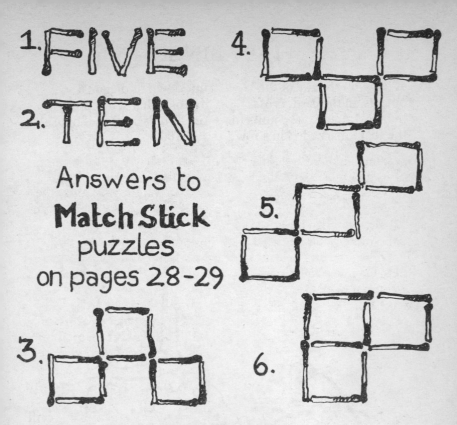

1. FIVE

2. TEN

Answers to
Match Stick
puzzles
on pages 28-29

3.

4.

5.

6.

SOUVENIRS

stamps
bus tickets
metro tickets
a policeman's fingerprint
matchboxes
sweet wrappers with French
  on them
marzipan animals and
  vegetables and fruit
feathers
wildflowers
stones and seashells and
  seaweed
postcards

French comics
menus
cheese labels
wine labels
fruit tissues with pictures
lump sugar wrappers with
  writing and pictures
rubbings from French coins
new kind of sweets

Collect as many of these as
you can. Get two of some of
the best things to give as
presents or bribes later.

I SPY BINGO

When you see any of the objects on the card, cross them off. Each one counts for the score marked. 3 in a row, up, down or diagonally, doubles that score. For finishing a card (full house) add 100.

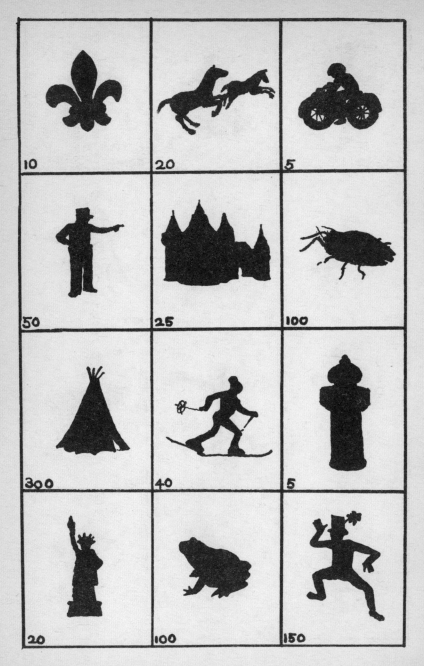

10

20

5

50

25

100

300

40

5

20

100

150

100   200   5

3   10   50

150   5   50

100   200   25